To GOD *be the* GLORY

Juden Zee

PAGE PUBLISHING
Conneaut Lake, PA

First originally published by Page Publishing 2023

ISBN 979-8-88960-053-4 (pbk)
ISBN 979-8-88960-066-4 (digital)

Printed in the United States of America

It was drizzling, and I was at the airport. I wanted to take a picture of my airplane. I saw a worker with a red cone. He guided the airplanes with his hand. I proceeded to take a picture. When I looked at the picture, I saw a *red heart* above the airplane, *smiley faces* on the different-colored raindrops, and a *white cross* underneath the airplane. *Thank you, Father God! Amen!*

I thought God used the red cone to make the *heart*. I told somebody, and they pointed out the cone. So God did it all by himself! Thank you, God! *Glory to God! Hallelujah! Amen.*

Many years ago, I purchased a Charlie Brown Christmas tree, and I wanted to decorate it the same way as on the video cassette cover. I wondered, *How will I find one red Christmas ornament?* I put my hand in the bag of Christmas ornaments, took *one* out, and it was *red*! *Glory to God! Amen!* When I turned the video cassette around, the Christmas tree was different, so I put the original Charlie Brown

Christmas tree away, and I got a fiber-optic Christmas tree. I was going to pop popcorn, then string it and decorate the Christmas tree like the video cassette back cover. Then I started taking pictures of the lighted Christmas tree. Then when I looked at the pictures I saw one was *twirled! Thank you, Father God!* So I didn't have to string popcorn. *To God be the glory! Thank you, God! Amen!*

Father God knows all. *Glory to God! Amen!* My grandson really likes dinosaurs. After my prayer, I looked up to the sky and saw a dinosaur. I hurried and took pictures because the clouds changed fast. An airplane and a part of the church were captured in the pictures below. *Glory to God!* Five months later, my grandson received the same dinosaur as a present on his birthday. *Thank you, Father God! Amen!*

At my mother's house, I saw rainbows next to her head, on her, and on the wall. I took pictures. My mother asked me if I saw rainbows at my house. I said no. Days later, I saw a rainbow in the sink. I took a picture. I moved the kitchen curtain, and on the windowsill I saw a small souvenir of Niagara Falls with a mirror and colored seashells, and I deleted the picture. When I went to my mother's house, I told her what happened. And I said, "There's something in your room that makes rainbows." I looked everywhere, but I didn't see anything. I told my mother, "If I see a rainbow at my house again, I will take a picture and I won't delete it."

At home, I prayed to see a rainbow in the sink. I was going to stay waiting no matter how long it took. It wasn't long before I saw a rainbow. Years later, at my daughter's house, she didn't have curtains in her living room window, and I saw a rainbow. I took a picture. *Thank you, God! Amen!*

At my mother's house, the home attendant told me to serve myself food. I said, "You only cook a little." She said, "Take! There's enough food." I thanked her and got a bowl and a fork. The home attendant pulled up a chair, and we were talking and looking at each other back and forth while I was serving myself. I looked for the smallest piece of *llami* (it's like a potato). Then I thought to take another piece of llami, looking for the smallest. Then in the other pot, I was looking for the smallest *bacalao* (I think that's cod fish).

I put it in the bowl. And when I looked at the bowl, I saw a smiley face. I said to my mother's home attendant, "Look at this," showing her the bowl. I thanked the Lord! I asked the home attendant to please write what she saw. The one llami came out with three dots across, the other piece of llami came out with three dots down, and the bacalao came out like a smile. And I saw the word *on* with a capital *N* and a period. *Glory to God! Thank you, Lord, for your miracle sign! Amen!*

In God we trust.

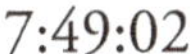

7:49:02

11-23:2018

Lo que paso fue increible. Juden, cohio dos piesas de llame y bacalao, y se formo en un plato y se puso una carita feliz con un capital N. Eso fue un milagro de Dios.

Gracias Amen.

Y yo Rosalba la home attendant de Laura, lo vi con mis ojos de lante de Dios.

7:48:30

7:47:38

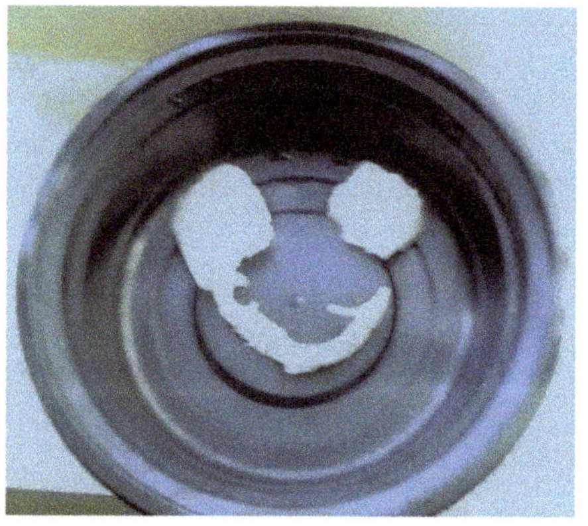

Rosalba wrote, "What happened was incredible. Juden took two pieces of llami and bacalao, and it formed a happy face with a capital *N*. That was a miracle from God. Thanks, amen. And I Rosalba, the home attendant of Laura, saw it with my eyes in front of God.

My daughter saw me having difficulty as there was one nail on the wall. I was trying to decorate, the wall had glossy paint, and I didn't have tape at that time. (Later, tape was bought.) I used stickers and also the airport name label that was on my suitcase. The decorations kept falling down. It took a while for the decorations to stay on the wall. Then when I took a picture of my grandson and I looked at it, I saw a bell. God did a miracle and put a bell in my grandson's birthday picture. Thank you, Father God! Glory to God! Amen! Hallelujah!

One day while I was walking, I saw something shine. I picked it up, and it was an apple. The leaf is a small diamond. That was what shined to my eyes. The apple represents the *apple of New York*! *Glory to God! Thank you, God! Amen!*

After I went to the store, pushing my shopping cart, I got home and began looking at pictures on my phone. I saw a picture of a floor. I didn't take that picture. Then I saw another picture of food items. I didn't take that picture either. Then I saw a *beautiful picture* of a dove. I didn't take that *miracle dove* picture either. God put that *miracle dove* picture on my phone! Thank you, Father God! Glory to God! Amen!

I tried to think of everywhere I went, and I went to several stores looking for the same floor. I don't know if I found it. Then I went to a 99¢ store, thinking maybe that was the store with the food items, but it wasn't. Then I went to Stop & Shop, and there they were—the same food items! I showed the manager the *beautiful dove picture* and the other pictures that were on my phone. I didn't take the pictures. I told him that God put the dove picture on my phone. That was a miracle sign from God. Glory to God. I asked the manager if he could please check the store camera because I didn't take a picture of food items. Then the nice manager checked the store camera, and he saw that I didn't take any pictures. Glory to God! Amen.

God put an angel on the Greyhound bus. He said my name. I asked him how he knew my name. He answered, "I saw you writing your name on the name tag." And he said his name was George. We became friends. He offered to buy me food, as all I was going to eat was chips. He bought my food. He told me that he told his work he going on the Greyhound bus, and he did. He then said that he saw a person with a surfboard and thought, *Ah, I know! I'm going to California.* At all bus stops, my angel George whom God gave me bought my food. I thank God! Glory to God! One time, God's angel George didn't think there was enough time to buy food. It was a short bus stop. I asked the bus driver if I had enough time to go to the store. And he said yes. I hurried to the store and bought food and drinks. My angel George smiled as I handed him the food and drink. On the Greyhound bus, there was a young lady. Her purse strap was broken. I told her I had several threaded needles, and I asked her if she wanted one. She said she didn't know how to sew. I asked her if she would like me to sew it for her. She said yes. I did. She was happy. She showed me a tattoo she said she recently got done, and she was almost in tears. She said she got a tattoo before, and it was okay. My angel George heard and saw. The next day, she said it didn't hurt anymore. We thanked God! My angel George asked me, "How is the young lady doing?" I said, "Fine." I thanked God the young lady said her tattoo didn't hurt anymore. My angel George told me to ask her if she would like to eat. I asked her, and she said yes. She gave my angel George a hug and thanked him. We all became friends. Pictures were taken with her phone, and when I looked at the pictures, I said, "Look! It looks like glamour shot pictures! Please take another picture of me." And she did.

I showed the pictures to somebody in New York, and they said there's something on that phone that makes you look younger. I told this to somebody else, and they said, "Then why is your face the only one that changed?" I said, "You're right! This is a *miracle from God*! Thank you, Lord! Amen!

I asked God's angel George if he wanted copies of the pictures. He said no. God's angel George didn't travel with a phone.

At one time, I said, "I don't even know your last name." God's angel George said, "You don't need to know that." At a bus terminal, God's angel George told me he changed his ticket going to Oregon. That's where I was going. When we got to the Oregon bus terminal, God's angel George asked me if I wanted to eat. Also, if my daughter would like to meet him and if she would like to eat. I called my daughter and told her all about God's angel George and everything.

I also asked if she wanted to meet him. She said she couldn't because she had to hurry back to work and said, "Thank you for everything." God's angel George took me to a restaurant, I told the waitress everything, and we all took a picture. I thanked God's angel George for everything, and I said I would always remember him. God's angel George smiled. Thank you, God! Glory to God! Amen! *Hallelujah!*

On a Greyhound bus, I met a young lady. I told her all about God's angel George and showed her pictures of *God's miracles*. She was happy. She got a phone call from her boyfriend. She told me that her boyfriend told her that her dog had puppies, but he didn't think one was going to make it. We prayed. When her boyfriend called her again, she told me that her boyfriend put the baby puppy next to the mother, and the baby puppy started drinking milk. She said she named the baby puppy George. She named him after *God's angel George! Thank you, God! Glory to God! Amen!*

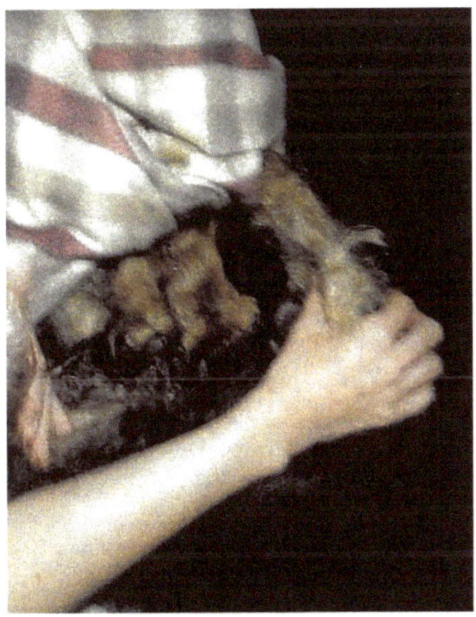

I told my grandson to get paper and crayons. My grandson said, "A rainbow, Grandma." I said, "Yes, and Grandma will draw a rainbow for you and send it to you, and Grandma will draw a rainbow for me." A friend paid for me to stay at a hotel. When I opened the door to my hotel room, I saw a rainbow rug. Thank you, God! Glory to God! Amen!

After pictures were taken, when I looked at the picture of me and my grandson, I saw a shadow of an apple on my pants. A sister's daughter from church also saw a rainbow at the top of the picture. I prayed, *What could this apple mean?* And it means, *the apple of New York*! *Thank you, God! Amen!*

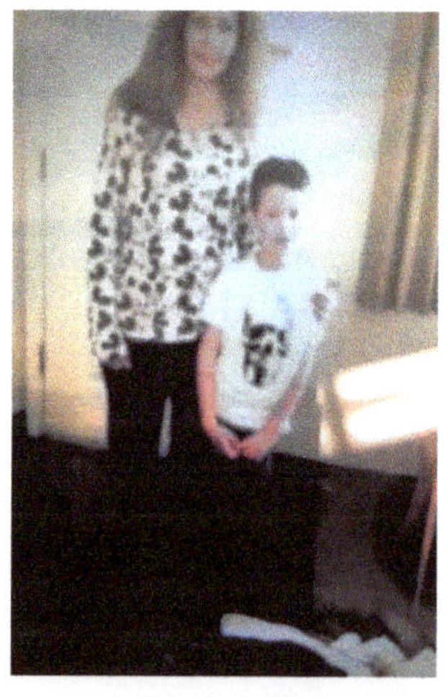

On the Greyhound bus, I saw a rainbow and what looked like a little dirt next to it. I took a picture. When I looked at it, I thought to make it big, and when I did, it turned out to be an apple. *Thank you, God! Glory to God! Amen!*

One day, I was visiting my family. We took pictures. I see a cross at the window next to my daughter's and my head. The lines on the window in this picture is not the same as the cross. *Thank you, God! Amen!*

I always give thanks to the Lord that my friend has helped me and paid for my airplane ticket for me to visit my family. Pictures were taken of me and my grandson, and our faces came out the same in each of the three pictures. Also, in the other two pictures, we came out alike. Thank you, God! Amen!

Also another time, when it was my flight date departure to take the airplane, I was lucky to sit next to a pilot, and I asked him for his autograph. And he said, yes. He said his name is spelled *E-l-i* but it's pronounced *LE*. Thank you, God! Amen! *Hallelujah!*

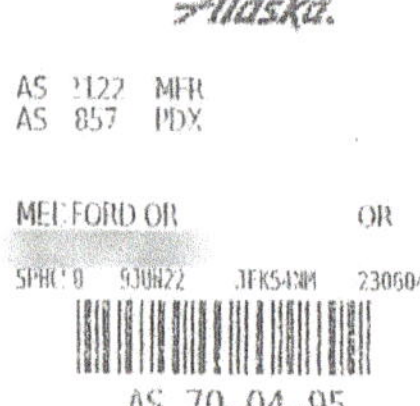

On my way going to the airport, I thank God all went well. It has always been an honor to meet my pilots. Also, a long time ago I thought to ask to get pictures taken with the pilots because if I wouldn't have asked, then I wouldn't have these wonderful pictures. Thank you, God! Amen!

Also years ago, I thanked God I was able to meet my pilots and have my picture taken with one of them. I also wore my sweater that says "My God is the CEO of the universe."

Also I wore the same sweater on the Greyhound bus when God's angel George whom God gave me took me to a restaurant, and we had our picture taken with the waitress.

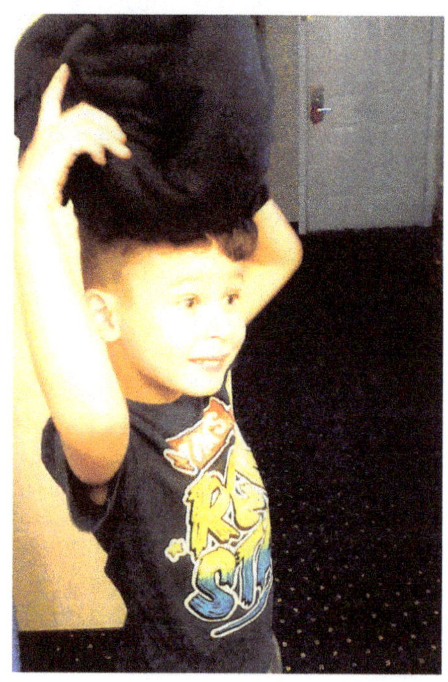

When my grandson was young, he rolled up my sweater that says "My God is the CEO of the universe," put it on his head, and smiled. I quickly got the camera and took a picture. Many years later, when I went to visit my grandson coming from New York to Oregon, I gave my grandson a balloon, and he put it on his head. I took a picture of me and my grandson.

On my way to my house in New York, I was lucky to meet the pilots, get their autographs, and get a picture taken with them.

Also many years ago, when my daughter was little we met a pilot at the airport, and we had our picture taken. Thank you, God! Amen!

Also, many years ago, when my daughter was little, we were lucky to meet the pilots.

We had our pictures taken, and we were lucky to go to the cockpit. My daughter was very happy and fascinated, and the pilot was very happy as he showed us all of the controllers of the airplane. Thank you, God! Also, we've had our sofa for many years. After looking at my grandson's picture with the balloon on his head, I looked at the sofa, and I noticed the wood of the sofa has a smiling face with a twirl on the head. It looks like the picture I took of my grandson when he rolled up my sweater that says "My God is the CEO of the universe," put it on his head, and smiled. Thank you, God! *Amen!*

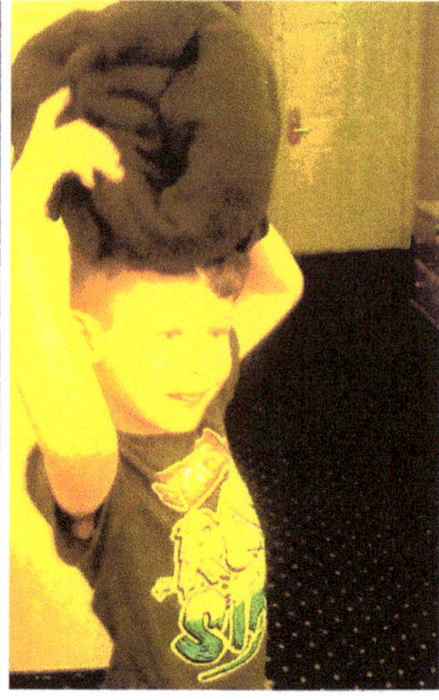

A long time ago, I thanked the Lord for touching my friend's heart because he paid for my airplane ticket for me to visit my family. While on the airplane, I asked somebody if they could take a picture of me giving thanks to God. They said yes, and I thanked them. *I gave thanks to my Father God for helping me and my family see each other. Thank you, Father God! Amen! Hallelujah!*

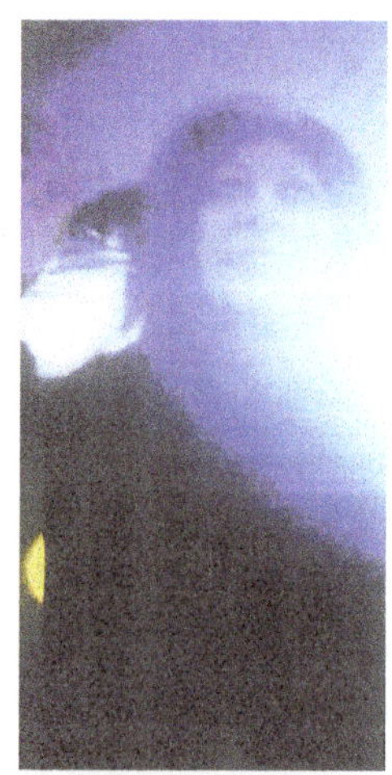

Thank you, Father God for always protecting me and all my family! And for giving me a lot of your miracle signs that made it possible for me to write this true book! I love you, Lord, and will always serve you!

Thank you! Amen!

About the Author

Juden Zee is a mother of two and has four grandchildren. She looks forward to future grandchildren and great-grandchildren, etc.

Mom loves you all very much!

www.ingramcontent.com/pod-product-compliance
Lightning Source LLC
Chambersburg PA
CBHW040120150726
48005CB00013B/1794